# Jane Goodall
## Chimpanzee Expert & Activist

by Grace Hansen

Clifton Park - Halfmoon Public Library
475 Moe Road
Clifton Park, New York 12065

ABDO
HISTORY MAKER
BIOGRAPHIES
Kids

**abdopublishing.com**

Published by Abdo Kids, a division of ABDO, PO Box 398166, Minneapolis, Minnesota 55439.

Copyright © 2015 by Abdo Consulting Group, Inc. International copyrights reserved in all countries. No part of this book may be reproduced in any form without written permission from the publisher.

Printed in the United States of America, North Mankato, Minnesota.

102014

012015

 THIS BOOK CONTAINS
RECYCLED MATERIALS

Photo Credits: AP Images, Corbis, Getty Images, Granger Collection, iStock, Landov Media, Shutterstock

Production Contributors: Teddy Borth, Jennie Forsberg, Grace Hansen

Design Contributors: Laura Rask, Dorothy Toth

Library of Congress Control Number: 2014943705

Cataloging-in-Publication Data

Hansen, Grace.

Jane Goodall: chimpanzee expert & activist / Grace Hansen.

p. cm. -- (History maker biographies)

Includes index. 2204

ISBN 978-1-62970-702-0

1. Goodall, Jane, 1934- --Juvenile literature. 2. Primatologists--England--Biography--Juvenile literature. 3. Women primatologists--England--Biography--Juvenile literature. 4. Chimpanzees--Tanzania--Gombe National Park--Juvenile literature. 1. Title.

599.8092--dc23

[B]

2014943705

# Table of Contents

## Early Life

Jane Goodall was born on April 3, 1934. She was born in London, England.

Asia

Europe

Africa

As a girl, Jane loved animals. She spent time playing and exploring. She dreamed of living in Africa.

6

Jane finished high school

in 1952. She could not

afford to go to college.

So she worked small jobs.

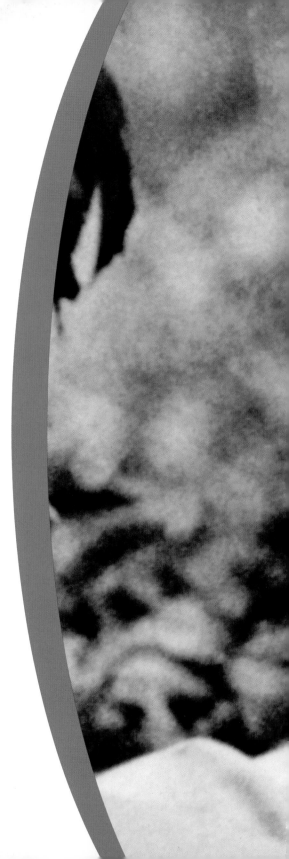

## To Africa!

In 1956, Jane was invited to Africa. Her friend's family had a farm in Kenya. Jane happily said yes.

In Africa, Jane met Dr. Louis Leakey. Jane helped him dig for **fossils**. Leakey gave her a new job. It was to study chimpanzees in Tanzania.

## Learning About Chimps

At first, the chimps ran away from Jane. So she watched from afar. In time, they let Jane get closer.

15

Jane learned many things about chimps. They used twigs as tools. They could be mean. More often, they were kind and loving.

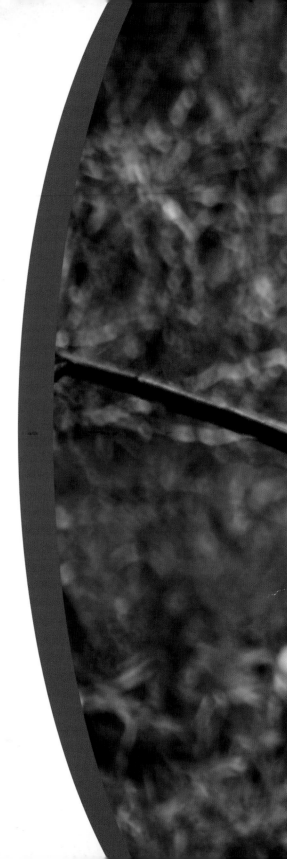

# Jane Goodall Institute

Jane knew chimps needed **protection**. In 1977, she started the Jane Goodall Institute. Its **mission** is to protect all living things.

18

## Jane Today

Today, Jane travels most of the year. She speaks to many people. She teaches them to make the world a better place.

21

# Timeline

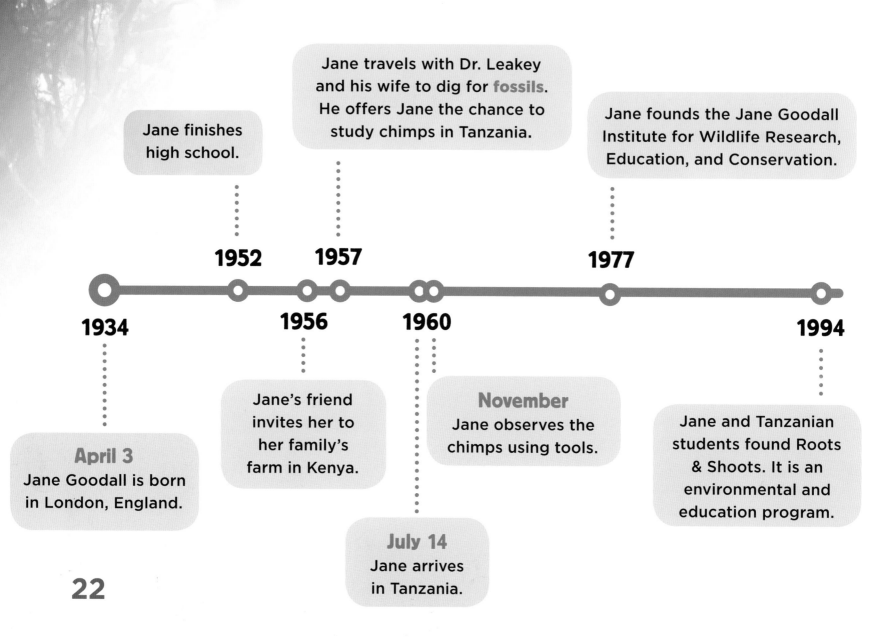

Jane finishes high school.

Jane travels with Dr. Leakey and his wife to dig for **fossils**. He offers Jane the chance to study chimps in Tanzania.

Jane founds the Jane Goodall Institute for Wildlife Research, Education, and Conservation.

**1952**

**1957**

**1977**

**1934**

**1956**

**1960**

**1994**

**April 3**
Jane Goodall is born in London, England.

Jane's friend invites her to her family's farm in Kenya.

**November**
Jane observes the chimps using tools.

Jane and Tanzanian students found Roots & Shoots. It is an environmental and education program.

**July 14**
Jane arrives in Tanzania.

# Glossary

**fossil** – the remains (skeleton, footprint, leaf, etc.) of something that existed a long time ago.

**mission** – a goal stated by a person, group, or business.

**protection** – the state of being kept from harm or loss.

# Index

# abdokids.com

Use this code to log on to abdokids.com and access crafts, games, videos, and more!

Abdo Kids Code:
HJK7020